Contents

KU-092-899

Any words appearing in the text in bold, **like this**, are explained in the Glossary.

Introducing molluscs

Molluscs form a large group (phylum) of **invertebrate** animals, the second largest after **arthropods**. There are about 100,000 known **species** of mollusc, found in a wide variety of marine, freshwater and land habitats.

There are seven classes of molluscs. The three main classes are **bivalves**, **gastropods** and **cephalopods**. Cephalopods are found only in the sea, but gastropods and bivalves live in marine and freshwater habitats. Some gastropods, such as slugs and garden snails, have **adapted** to live on land and cannot live in water. The aplacophorans, monoplacophorans, scaphopods and polyplacophorans form the minor classes (see pages 36–37).

▶ More than three-quarters of molluscs are gastropods. The soft body and prominent tentacles of this slug are **characteristic** mollusc features.

Appearance

Molluscs differ greatly in appearance, although they do share a basic body plan. Most molluscs have a well-developed head, with **tentacles** and eyes. The head is usually joined to a flat, muscular foot. Above the foot, the body organs are contained in a hump covered by a sheet of tissue called the **mantle**. There is also a space, called the **mantle cavity** between the mantle and the rest of the body. This has a different purpose in different types of mollusc.

Classification key

KINGDOM	Animalia
PHYLUM	**Mollusca**
CLASSES	7 – Aplacophora (worm-shaped solenogasters and deep-sea worm-like Caudofoveata), Polyplacophora (chitons), Monoplacophora, Bivalvia (cockles, clams and mussels), Scaphopoda (tusk shells), Gastropoda (snails and slugs), Cephalopoda (octopuses, cuttlefish, squid and nautiluses)
ORDERS	35
FAMILIES	about 232
SPECIES	over 100,000

Molluscs

Ruth Miller

Raintree

www.raintreepublishers.co.uk

Visit our website to find out more information about **Raintree** books.

To order:
 Phone 44 (0) 1865 888113
Send a fax to 44 (0) 1865 314091
Visit the Raintree Bookshop at **www.raintreepublishers.co.uk** to browse our catalogue and order online.

Produced for Raintree by
White-Thomson Publishing Ltd
Bridgewater Business Centre, 210 High Street,
Lewes, East Sussex, BN7 2NH

First published in Great Britain by
Raintree, Halley Court, Jordan Hill, Oxford OX2 8EJ,
part of Harcourt Education.
Raintree is a registered trademark of Harcourt Education Ltd.

© Harcourt Education Ltd 2005
First published in paperback in 2006
The moral right of the proprietor has been asserted.

Consultant: Dr Rod Preston-Mafham
Editorial: Katie Orchard, Nick Hunter and Catherine Clarke
Design: Tim Mayer
Picture Research: Morgan Interactive Ltd
Production: Amanda Meaden

Originated by Dot Gradations Ltd
Printed in China by WKT Company Limited

ISBN 1 844 43769 8 (hardback) ISBN 1 844 43779 5 (paperback)
09 08 07 06 05   10 09 08 07 06
10 9 8 7 6 5 4 3 2 1   10 9 8 7 6 5 4 3 2 1

British Library Cataloguing in Publication Data
Miller, Ruth
Molluscs. – (Animal Kingdom)
594
A full catalogue record for this book is available from the British Library

Acknowledgements
The publishers would like to thank the following for permission to reproduce photographs: Corbis pp. **8**, **13**, **15** bottom, **24** bottom (Brandon Cole), **30**, **48**; Digital Vision **Title**, **Contents** (main), pp. **4**, **5** background, **21** bottom, **42**, **44** bottom, **45**; Ecoscene **Contents** left and right (Jeff Collett), pp. **6** (John Lewis), **9** bottom (Kjell Sandved), **10** (John Lewis), **11** bottom (Kevin King), **18** (Reinhard Dirscherl), **22**, **23** (Kjell Sandved), **26**, **27** bottom (Jeff Collett), **29** top (Reinhard Dirscherl), **31** left (John Lewis), **32** (Reinhard Dirscherl), **38-39** Jeff Collett, **39** top (Alan Towse), **40** (John Liddiard), **43** (Kevin King), **44** top (Frank Blackburn); Ecoscene-Papilio pp. **5** top, **15**, **34** (Robert Pickett); Nature Photo Library pp. **9** top (Jason Smalley), **12** top (Jeff Foott), **27** top (Georgette Douwma); NHPA pp. **7** top (Paal Hermansen), **7** bottom (Linda Pitkin), **12** (Norbert Wu), **14** (Stephen Dalton), **16** (Roy Waller), **17** right (Matt Bain), **17** left (Laurie Campbell), **19** top (Patrick O'Neill), **19** bottom (B Jones and M Shimlock), **20** (Robert Thompson), **21** top (Stephen Dalton), **23** top (B Jones and M Shimlock), **23** bottom (G Bernard), **24** top (Trevor MacDonald), **25** top (Roy Waller), **28** top (B Jones and M Shimlock), **31** right (ANT), **33** top (Bill Wood), **33** bottom (B Jones and M Shimlock), **35** bottom (Daniel Heuclin), **36** right (G Bernard), **39** bottom (Roy Waller), **41** top (G Bernard), **41** bottom (Nigel Callow); Photodisc pp. **5** bottom, **11** top, **28–29**, **35** top, **46**; Patrick Reynolds p. **37**.

Front cover photograph of snails reproduced with permission of Corbis (Anthony Bannister/ Gallo). Back cover image of a snail is reproduced with permission of Getty Images.

Every effort has been made to contact copyright holders of any material reproduced in this book. Any omissions will be rectified in subsequent printings if notice is given to the publishers.

The paper used to print this book comes from sustainable resources.

Aquatic molluscs (those that live in water), such as the edible mussel, have **gills** in their mantle cavity. In land molluscs, the cavity forms a **lung**. In molluscs that have shells, the mantle produces the materials that make the shell.

Some molluscs, such as bivalves, are filter feeders and get their food from the water in which they live. They use their gills to trap tiny **organisms**. Many gastropods and cephalopods have a rough tongue-like structure in the mouth. This structure is covered with rows of tiny, sharp teeth, which are used to scrape particles of food into the mouth.

▲ The octopus is a cephalopod. The prominent head is surrounded by the foot. The tentacles (often referred to as arms) are formed from the front part of the foot and have powerful suckers, which are used to capture **prey**.

A hard shell surrounds the hump containing body organs.

The head has well-developed tentacles and eyes.

The flat, muscular foot allows the mollusc to move around.

▲ The snail is a land gastropod.

Classification

Living organisms are classified, or organized, according to how closely related one organism is to another. The basic group in classification is the species, for example humans belong to the species *Homo sapiens*. A species is a group of individuals that are similar to each other and that can **interbreed** with one another. Species are grouped together into genera (singular: genus). A genus may contain a number of species that share some features. *Homo* is the human genus. Genera are grouped together in families, the families grouped into orders and the orders grouped into classes. Classes are grouped together in phyla (singular: phylum) and finally the phyla are grouped into kingdoms. Kingdoms are the largest groups. Molluscs belong to the phylum Mollusca, in the animal kingdom. (To find out more see pages 42–43.)

Mollusc life cycle and behaviour

Molluscs have a wide variety of body forms, from slugs to giant squid. In most molluscs, the egg hatches into a **larval** stage (an early stage of development between **fertilized** egg and adult). **Aquatic** molluscs have free-swimming larvae. In some aquatic **species**, the egg hatches into a simple larva that is covered in tiny hairs, or **cilia**. This is called a trochophore larva. This stage quickly develops into a more complex veliger larva, which has many adult features including a head, a foot and a tiny shell. In other species, this development takes place inside the egg and the veliger larva emerges on hatching. In land molluscs, such as snails, and **cephalopods**, such as octopuses, all the larval stages take place within the egg before hatching.

Males and females

Some molluscs, such as snails, are **hermaphrodites**, which means that individuals have both male and female sex organs. Others, such as mussels and cephalopods, have separate sexes. Some **bivalves** and **gastropods** can change sex during their lifetimes. For example, oysters are bivalves that may mature as males before becoming female and producing eggs. After the eggs have been released, the oyster becomes a male again.

▼ There are no larval stages in the life cycle of the cuttlefish, so the young hatch as miniature adults. Even when young, the eyes are very prominent.

The garden snail

The common garden snail, *Helix aspersa*, is a hermaphrodite gastropod. In this species, **mating** results in the exchange of male sex cells between partners. Two snails circle each other, touching each other with their **tentacles**, before becoming entwined. The sex cells are then exchanged and stored inside each snail's body until the eggs are laid a few weeks later. The eggs are usually laid in small batches of about 50, in damp soil. The tough shells each contain a yolk. Inside the eggs, the larval stages develop and the eggs grow bigger. After a week or two, the young snails hatch.

▲ When slugs, such as these black slugs, mate, they twist around each other and produce large quantities of sticky mucus.

Amazing facts

- The courtship of the great grey slug can last for over an hour. Two slugs circle each other, producing large amounts of **mucus**. They crawl up a wall or tree trunk and mate in mid-air at the end of a string of sticky mucus.
- A female octopus can lay 150,000 eggs in a week.

Cephalopod life cycles

Cuttlefish are a group of cephalopods in which the sexes are separate. After courtship, mating occurs and the female's eggs are laid singly, each being attached to seaweed or **coral** by a thread. Miniature cuttlefish hatch from these fertilized eggs.

After a female octopus has laid her eggs, she looks after them for several weeks. She keeps them clean with her arms and blows water over them. During the time she spends looking after the eggs, she does not eat and may die soon afterwards.

◀ During courtship, the male cuttlefish develops a striped pattern on his body and swims around above the female, before depositing a sac of sperm into her **mantle cavity**.

Feeding methods

Molluscs have a wide range of feeding methods. There are **carnivores**, **herbivores** and **omnivores**. Some molluscs are **parasites**, feeding on **host** animals without killing them.

▲ The octopus is a predator and can hold on to its prey using the powerful suckers on its tentacles.

Browsers and grazers

The **browsers** and **grazers**, such as snails and limpets, use their **radulae** to scrape food into their mouths. The radula is a **membrane** that covers a tongue-like structure called the odontophore that is fixed to the floor of the mouth. The radula has many rows of tiny teeth, which curve backwards into the mouth. The mollusc pushes the odontophore out of its mouth and uses the radula like rough sandpaper to tear off pieces of food. The radula is then withdrawn into the mouth. Here, saliva containing **mucus** sticks the food particles together. Other substances in the saliva begin to break down, or digest, the food.

Filter feeders

Filter feeding is a **characteristic** of **bivalves** such as mussels. Bivalves do not have a distinct head or a radula. They do have well-developed **gills**, called ctenidia, in the **mantle cavity** inside the shell. These gills are covered in tiny hairs, called **cilia**. The gills act as strainers. The cilia beat rhythmically, creating a current of water which brings in tiny food particles. Mucus on the gills traps the particles and is moved to the mouth by the cilia, where it is passed into the digestive system.

Amazing facts

- The radula of a browsing mollusc is continually worn away through use. Special cells produce rows of teeth at the back of the radula. As the new teeth form, the whole structure moves forward, towards the front of the mouth.
- The venom of a cone shell can be fatal to humans. It is similar to curare, a poison that oozes from certain South American trees and is used to make poison arrows.

Predators

Cephalopods, such as the octopus, are **predators**. The head is surrounded by **tentacles** or arms, which have suckers on them for catching and holding **prey**. The mouth has a pair of strong jaws that form a beak-like structure. Inside the mouth, there is a radula and two pairs of salivary glands. One pair of these glands makes **venom**, which is injected into the prey as it is bitten by the jaws.

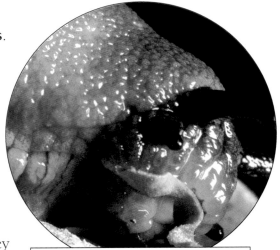

Some **gastropods** are predators. Cone shells feed on worms, other molluscs or small fish. They follow the scent of their prey and then use long, sharp teeth to bite and inject it with venom. The paralysed victim is then swallowed whole. Once a tooth has been used, it usually breaks off and another is brought forward from the radula for use on the next victim.

▲ Slugs are grazers and use their radula to tear off pieces of plant material.

Some gastropods, such as dog whelks, use their radula to bore holes into the shells of other molluscs. Worm shells produce mucus from their foot. The mucus traps small animals on which the worm shells feed.

▼ Bivalves, such as this file shell, are filter feeders. They draw water containing food particles over their gills. The particles are trapped by sticky mucus and then swallowed.

Mollusc classes

Most members of the **mollusc** phylum have an external shell. In many groups, the shell provides shape and protection for the soft body. Some shells are **adapted** for burrowing, while others are patterned and **camouflage** their owners so that they can avoid **predators**.

Single shells

Gastropods are the largest group of molluscs that have a single external shell. Examples include the abalone, the cone shell and the garden snail. In this class, the shell is usually coiled into a spiral, into which the animal can withdraw its body. Many **aquatic** gastropods have an **operculum**, a plate that closes and seals the opening of the shell, protecting the animal inside. Slugs have either a very small shell, or no shell at all. Gastropods are found all over the world in marine, freshwater and land habitats. They range in size from less than 0.1 to more than 25 centimetres long.

Amazing facts

- Some of the largest gastropods are sea slugs. They can weigh up to about 20 kilograms, which is about three times the weight of an average domestic cat.

- The largest bivalves found today are giant clams, found in the **coral** reefs of the Indian and Pacific Oceans. They can weigh more than 200 kilograms.

- The gastropod with the largest shell is the Australian Trumpet, a snail found in northern Australia. Its shell can be up to 60 centimetres across.

◀ Volute shells have distinctive markings. These gastropods are slow-moving **carnivores**, spending much of their time buried in mud. They smother **prey** with their large foot.

▼ The single shell of the garden snail stops it from drying out and protects it from predators.

Scaphopods, or tusk shells, (see pages 36–37) also have single shells, but differ from gastropods in several ways. The shells of scaphopods are long, tubular structures that are open at both ends. The shells look like curved tusks, with one end wider than the other. Scaphopods do not have eyes, **tentacles** or **gills**. They live in oceans and range in size from 0.2 to 15 centimetres long.

Monoplacophorans (see pages 36–37) are adapted for living at great depths in the oceans, where there is less competition for food and living space from other **species**. They have a cone-shaped shell and no eyes or tentacles. There are very few species, and they range in size from 0.2 to 3.5 centimetres in length.

Two shells – the bivalves

Bivalves, such as the edible mussel, have a shell in two parts, or valves. The two valves are joined together by a tough, flexible **ligament**. The body usually consists of a foot, which is flattened like a wedge, and a large **mantle cavity** containing prominent gills. They have no head and no **radula**. Many adult bivalves live attached to rocks and do not move around. They are filter feeders, obtaining their food by drawing a current of water through their bodies (see pages 8–9).

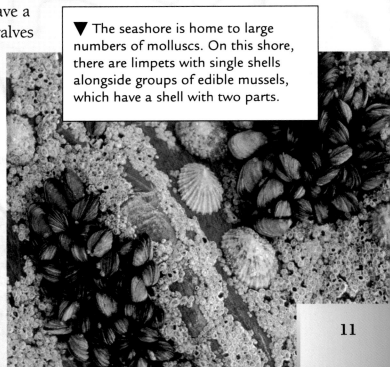

▼ The seashore is home to large numbers of molluscs. On this shore, there are limpets with single shells alongside groups of edible mussels, which have a shell with two parts.

Chitons

Chitons belong to the order Polyplacophora (see pages 36–37) and have external shells made up of eight plates, which often overlap. There is a well-developed foot, a head, and **gills** that allow the chiton to take in oxygen. There are no eyes or **tentacles**, but some **species** have sensors in their shells that detect changes in light. A chiton uses its foot to move from one place to another and for clinging on to rocks. If it is detached from the rock, it can roll up into a ball. All chitons are marine, many living on rocky shores and some living in quite deep water. They are **grazers**, using their **radula** to scrape algae from rock surfaces.

▲ The overlapping plates of the chiton's shell can clearly be seen in this photograph.

No external shells

The class Aplacophora (see pages 36–37) contains worm-like **molluscs** without shells. They do not look much like other molluscs as they do not have a foot and the head is poorly developed, but they do have a radula. The body is surrounded by a tough covering containing tiny pieces of chalky material. These molluscs are found on the seabed, burrowing through the sediment and feeding on small animals or their remains.

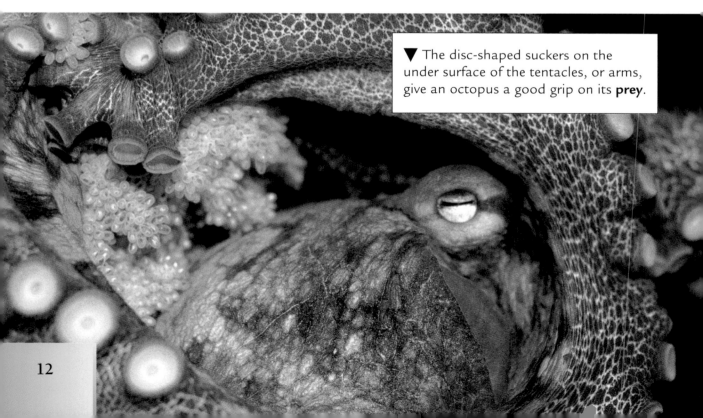

▼ The disc-shaped suckers on the under surface of the tentacles, or arms, give an octopus a good grip on its **prey**.

Cephalopods

The **characteristic** feature of **cephalopods** is the presence of tentacles, or arms, surrounding the mouth. The only cephalopods to have true external shells are nautiluses (see pages 34–35). Cuttlefish, squid and octopuses, have either an internal shell or no shell. Cephalopods vary greatly in shape. Most are **streamlined** and their foot forms a funnel, which can remove water rapidly from the **mantle cavity**. The water is pushed out like a jet, so some of these molluscs can move very quickly. Many cephalopods can change colour and some can produce an ink-like substance when they are threatened by a **predator**. The ink makes the water cloudy, hiding the cephalopod from the predator and allowing it to escape.

A primitive mollusc

Using knowledge of the features of living molluscs, scientists have tried to work out what the **ancestor** of modern molluscs would have looked like. It is quite likely that this ancient relative lived in shallow seas, crawled over rocks and fed on algae. These creatures were probably small, oval in shape and protected by a shell, which could be clamped down on to the rocks. They are thought to have been able to crawl using a muscular foot. They were able to scrape their food from the rocks using their radula. The modern limpet would be the closest living mollusc to this **primitive** ancestor.

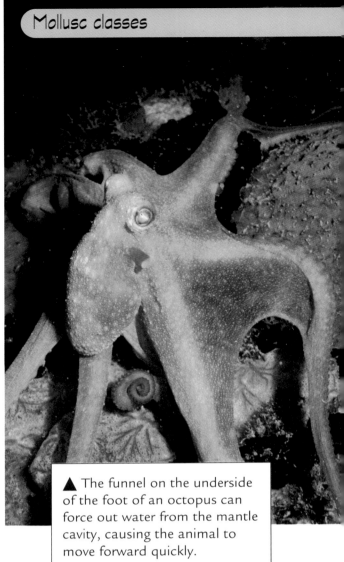

▲ The funnel on the underside of the foot of an octopus can force out water from the mantle cavity, causing the animal to move forward quickly.

Amazing facts

- The marbled chiton is found in large numbers (up to 50 per square metre) on the rocks and stones of Scottish sea lochs.
- The body of the blind deep-sea octopus is like that of a jellyfish. It is so transparent that the page of a newspaper can be read through it.

Gastropods

About 80 per cent of all **molluscs** are **gastropods**. They range in size from tiny snails to large sea slugs that can weigh up to 13 kilograms. Gastropods are found in marine, freshwater and land habitats all over the world. A typical gastropod has a single shell, a muscular foot, a well-developed head with eyes and **tentacles**, and a **radula**. The shell is usually coiled into a spiral, although in slugs it is small, or there is no shell.

Gastropods are divided into three sub-classes: prosobranchs, opisthobranchs and pulmonates. Prosobranchs are the oldest group. The other two groups are thought to have **evolved** from this one.

Aquatic gastropods

Most gastropods are prosobranchs and have typical gastropod features. Prosobranchs, such as limpets and cone shells, are mostly found in marine habitats, although there are some land-dwelling and freshwater **species**. Prosobranchs have only one pair of tentacles on the head and their eyes are at the base of these tentacles. Opisthobranchs are all marine animals. The more **primitive** members of the group have coiled shells, but in many species the shell is small or there is no shell. Some species are brightly coloured and have external **gills**.

Classification key

PHYLUM	Mollusca
CLASS	**Gastropoda**
SUB-CLASSES	3 – Prosobranchia (abalones, limpets and cone shells), Opisthobranchia (sea hares, sea slugs and bubble shells) and Pulmonata (land snails and slugs)
ORDERS	15
SPECIES	about 75,000

▼ The leopard slug is a gastropod without a shell. It gets its name from its distinctive markings.

14

▲ Ramshorn snails are pulmonates that live in fresh water. They breathe air and can survive in stagnant water that has a low oxygen content as well as in fast-flowing streams.

Pulmonates

Pulmonates can be separated from the other two major groups of gastropods as they do not have an **operculum** or gills. The **mantle cavity** has **adapted** to form a **lung**. Pulmonates have two pairs of tentacles. The eyes are located at the ends of the longer pair of tentacles. The shorter pair of tentacles can detect smells and help the mollusc to find its food. Many land pulmonates have external shells, which may be patterned or brightly coloured. Some land slugs have internal shells, but they are very small and contained within the **mantle**.

Amazing facts

- 'Gastropod' means 'stomach foot' and refers to the position of the stomach immediately above the muscular foot.
- Garden snails move at speeds of around 0.06 kilometres (0.04 miles) per hour.
- The Romans fattened snails for food by feeding them on bran soaked in wine.

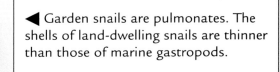

◄ Garden snails are pulmonates. The shells of land-dwelling snails are thinner than those of marine gastropods.

Marine gastropods

The distribution of marine **gastropods** is linked to their food supply. The **browsers** and **grazers**, such as limpets and top shells, feed on seaweed or other small algae. They are therefore found on rocky shores, in rock pools or in shallow coastal waters, where there is enough light for these plants to grow. Light cannot reach the deeper waters, so there are no plants available. **Predatory** gastropods, such as **venomous** cone shells and some sea slugs, are found mostly in shallow coastal waters and **coral** reefs, where there is plenty of food. Some **species**, such as dog whelks, are found in the **intertidal zone** (the area of the shore that is covered and exposed by the tides), **preying** on other gastropods and **arthropods**.

Classification key	
SUB-CLASS	Prosobranchia
ORDERS	4
FAMILIES	51
SPECIES	7000

Rocky shores

Rocky shores are very specialized habitats, usually with clear zones of vegetation associated with different prosobranch gastropods. In the UK, for example, the black periwinkle and the rough periwinkle graze on lichens and tiny algae in the splash zone, the area of the shore furthest from the sea. They have thick, tough shells, which protect them from waves and from drying out. They can survive extremes of temperature and attach themselves firmly to the rocks when the sea is at its roughest. If they are dislodged from their rocks by waves and washed down the shore towards the sea, they move back up to their previous positions.

▼ Blue-rayed limpets are small marine gastropods that graze on seaweed, called kelp, on the seashore.

In the middle of the intertidal zone, the flat periwinkle is found feeding on bladderwrack (a type of seaweed). This periwinkle cannot survive in the conditions higher up the shore, but is well **adapted** to living on the seaweed of the middle shore. It is covered by the tide for longer and the temperature is less variable.

Limpets are **herbivores** that have adapted to cope with conditions on the middle and lower regions of rocky shores. These areas of the shore are covered by the tide for longer. The limpets rotate their shells on the rock surface and grind out a dent (a 'home scar') into which they fit. Each limpet has its own scar to which it returns after grazing. At low tide, the muscular foot clamps down firmly to the surface of the rocks, so that water is not lost and the limpet is protected from predators and waves.

▼ Dog whelks eat other molluscs such as mussels, limpets and barnacles.

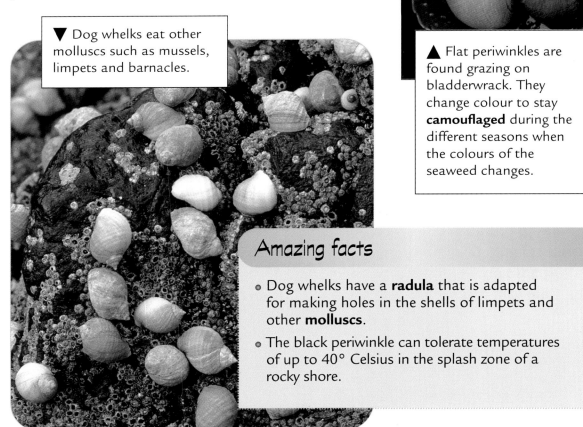

▲ Flat periwinkles are found grazing on bladderwrack. They change colour to stay **camouflaged** during the different seasons when the colours of the seaweed changes.

Amazing facts

- Dog whelks have a **radula** that is adapted for making holes in the shells of limpets and other **molluscs**.
- The black periwinkle can tolerate temperatures of up to 40° Celsius in the splash zone of a rocky shore.

Sea slugs

Sea slugs and their relatives are **gastropods** that have little or no shell. The most **primitive** groups have coiled shells, but most adult sea slugs have no shells. The major groups of sea slugs include bubble shells, sea hares, sacoglossans, side-**gilled** slugs and nudibranchs (naked gills).

The shell of a sea hare is simply a horny structure embedded in the **mantle**, and it is not visible. The North Atlantic sea hare crawls around on the seabed amongst the seaweed. It can swim using flaps along the sides of its body and grows up to 30 centimetres long.

Nudibranchs are very colourful marine gastropods that can be divided into two groups – dorids and eolids. Dorids are oval-shaped and have feathery gills on their backs. Eolids are more elongated and have no gills. On their backs they have outgrowths of fine tubes, called cerata. The cerata contain stinging cells, which the eolids obtain from the **sea anemones** and jellyfish that they eat. When an eolid is attacked, it can sting its attacker using these sting cells.

▲ This brightly coloured dorid nudibranch is oval in shape and has a large number of feathery gills on its back.

Rocky shores

The sea lemon has a mottled yellowish body and is sometimes found on the lower rocky shores of the UK in the summer months. It feeds on the breadcrumb sponge, which grows under boulders. The grey sea slug is commonly found under stones on the shore and it feeds on sea anemones.

◀ This sea lemon is feeding on a breadcrumb sponge.

Classification key

PHYLUM	Mollusca
CLASS	Gastropoda
SUB-CLASS	**Opisthobranchia**
ORDERS	9
FAMILIES	107
GENERA	168
SPECIES	approximately 2000

Amazing facts

- The largest nudibranch in the world is the orange peel nudibranch, which can reach 30 centimetres in length. It feeds on orange sea pens and soft coral.
- When disturbed, the sea hare can squirt a violet dye into the water. This hides it from its enemies for a few moments, giving it time to escape.

Coral reefs

Many sea slugs live on **coral** reefs. Some feed on the corals, but others are **herbivores**. The lettuce sea slug is a saccoglossan. It feeds on algae that grow on the reef. The teeth on the **radula** slice open the cells of the algae and suck up the sap. The green substance in the sap is stored in the slug's digestive system, making it look green. This substance, called chlorophyll, is used by the algae to trap energy from sunlight and make food for the plant. It continues to work once it is inside the sea slug.

▲ The lettuce slug is **camouflaged** to look like a leaf. It has no shell and breathes through its skin.

Land gastropods

Land **gastropods** include garden snails and slugs. Snails all have external shells. Some slugs have small, internal shells and one group, called semi-slugs, have a tiny external shell perched on the end of the foot. The shells of most land snails are **camouflaged** so that they can blend in with their surroundings and avoid **predators**.

Most land gastropods are active at night. Their bodies lose moisture easily and they need water to make **mucus**, the slime that helps them to move smoothly. During the day, snails withdraw into their shells and stick themselves to the undersides of pots, stones or logs, to reduce water loss. Slugs squeeze themselves into small spaces under bark and into gaps between paving stones.

Land gastropods do not have **gills**. The **mantle cavity** is **adapted** to form a **lung**. Air is drawn into the mantle cavity through an external opening, called the pneumostome, which can also be closed to reduce water loss.

Classification key	
PHYLUM	Mollusca
CLASS	Gastropoda
SUB-CLASS	**Pulmonata**
ORDER	4
FAMILIES	36
GENERA	103

Survival strategies

During very dry weather and in cold winters, snails seal the opening of their shell with a layer of mucus which becomes hard and waterproof. Inside the sealed shell, the snail can survive for several months. Snails that live in warmer climates, where the ground becomes hot in summer, climb up into the vegetation. Then they close off the opening to their shells so that they do not lose too much water. This behaviour is called **aestivation** and means that the snails are able to survive until conditions become more favourable. Slugs usually burrow underground when conditions are dry.

◀ The sticky mucus produced by this kerry slug protects the foot as it crawls over the ground.

◀ The shell of the banded snail is camouflaged so that it blends in with the vegetation in which it lives.

Moving around on land

Slugs and snails, like all gastropods, move by means of wave-like contractions of the muscles in the foot. As the muscles tighten, they pull the flat part of the foot into a series of tiny ridges, pushing the animal forwards. Mucus is produced from special glands on the bottom of the foot. The mucus helps the snail or slug slide along the ground and protects the soft tissues of the foot from being damaged by sharp stones. The mucus is very sticky and helps the gastropods to grip surfaces, so that they can climb up walls and over objects.

Amazing facts

- Slugs were once used as a cure for warts. The wart was rubbed with the slug and then the slug was impaled on a thorn. The wart was supposed to disappear as the slug died and withered.
- The largest land snail is the giant African land snail whose extended body can reach a length of 20 centimetres.

▶ The moss on this rock is providing a good supply of food for this snail.

21

Bivalves

Bivalves are found in marine and freshwater habitats all over the world. They range in size from tiny clams about 0.5 millimetres long to the giant clam, which can grow to lengths of more than 1 metre. Their main **characteristic** is a shell made up of two halves, or valves, joined by a hinge.

◄ The cockle is more spherical than many bivalves, with the two valves very similar in shape. Ridges form a fan-like pattern on each half of the shell.

Two halves

The two valves of the bivalve shell are held together by a flexible, tough **ligament**. The valves can be closed by powerful muscles attached to the inside of the shell. When the bivalve is at rest, the muscles are relaxed and the valves are open. Usually there are two sets of these muscles, but scallops have only a single, central set.

Bivalve features

Bivalves do not have a head or a **radula**. There are often simple sense organs, which are sensitive to touch and to differences in light. These are found on small **tentacles** along the edges of the **mantle**. Bivalves are filter feeders (see page 8). Food particles are trapped in **mucus** on the ctenidia, or **gills**. The food is then transferred to a pair of **appendages**, called labial palps, which push it into the mouth. Most bivalves feed on tiny algae and animals, and on the decaying remains of plants and animals.

Classification key	
PHYLUM	Mollusca
CLASS	**Bivalvia**
ORDERS	10
FAMILIES	114
SPECIES	about 15,000

◀ The shells of edible oysters are often covered with other marine animals and plants.

Bivalves have a muscular foot, but it is wedge-shaped and not used to glide along as it is in **gastropods**. It is either used for attachment or for burrowing. In some bivalves, such as mussels, the foot produces threads, called byssal threads. These are made of tough protein and anchor the mussel to the rocks. Others, such as cockles, use their foot for burrowing into soft sand.

Most bivalves use their ctenidia to take in oxygen, which they need for their essential body functions, and for trapping food. A current of water is drawn across the surface of the ctenidia so that oxygen can be absorbed. The water is drawn into the animal by a muscular tube called the inhalant **siphon**. The water passes over the ctenidia and then leaves through another tube called the exhalant siphon.

Amazing facts

- Scallops can swim away from danger, opening and closing their shells to push themselves along, but most bivalves shut themselves up inside their shells for protection.
- The spiny cockle can leap distances of up to 10 centimetres if its shell is touched by a **predator** such as a starfish.

▼ Bivalves such as mussels open under water to show the edges of the mantle.

Rock busters

Piddocks live in burrows. They have bean-shaped shells with rough teeth on the front edges of the valves. As their bodies twist and turn, they open and close their shells in order to drill burrows in solid rock. The outer layers of the shell are worn away by the drilling, so the piddock moves its **mantle** over the worn shell and makes a new layer. Date mussels can also insert themselves into solid rock, but they do not use the same method as piddocks. Instead of drilling their way in, they produce chemicals that dissolve the rock. They can be found in the hard **coral** reefs of the Red Sea.

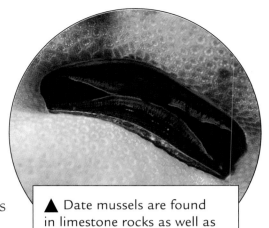

▲ Date mussels are found in limestone rocks as well as in coral reefs.

A diet of sawdust

Shipworms can make holes in wooden structures, such as the hulls of boats and the underwater foundations of jetties. These **bivalves** feed on the sawdust from the wood they drill out. Their bodies are elongated and worm-like, with the shell reduced to two small valves at the front end of the animal. These valves act like a drill to bore into the wood. The mantle covers the body behind the shell and forms a hard, chalky tube in which the shipworm lives. Shipworms are more common in warm waters, where their bodies may grow to over 2 metres in length.

▼ The piddock can drill its way into rock using the sharp edges of the two parts of its shell.

Sand burrowers

The common razor shell, *Ensis ensis*, is found on sandy shores. It grows to about 13 centimetres long and is able to burrow into the sand quickly with its flexible, muscular foot. When burrowing, the foot is elongated and pushed down into the sand as far as it will go. The tip of the foot swells and anchors the razor shell. The foot muscles then tighten and pull the shell down into the sand. This action is repeated until the animal is completely buried.

The soft-shelled clam or steamer clam is found burrowing in areas of sand and mud in the **intertidal zone** of the shore. It has thin, fragile valves that are up to 15 centimetres long, and it is usually found about 10–30 centimetres below the surface. Soft-shelled clams may live for up to 12 years.

▶ The elongated foot of the razor shell enables it to burrow quickly into soft sand.

Amazing facts

- Razor shells, or razor clams, are dug out of the sand as food for humans. They are located by the dent left on the surface of the sand, where the shell has been pulled down.
- Shipworms can make holes 2 centimetres wide in the bottoms of wooden boats.

The giant clam

The giant clam is the largest **bivalve mollusc**, growing up to
1 metre in diameter. It is found in the Pacific and Indian Oceans,
and is most common in the warm waters of shallow lagoons and flat
areas in **coral** reefs. It can live at depths of up to 20 metres.

Giant clams stay fixed in one place. Their shells are thick and
heavy and they lie with their hinge downwards on the seabed. The
mantle may be golden brown, yellow or green, with purple, blue or
green spots around the edges. There are also pale or
clear spots, called 'windows', on the mantle. If the
clams are disturbed, the brightly coloured mantle
tissue is withdrawn inside the shell and the valves
close together.

Classification key

PHYLUM	Mollusca
CLASS	Bivalvia
ORDER	Veneroida
FAMILY	Tridacnidae
GENUS	*Tridacna*
SPECIES	***Tridacna gigas***

Feeding

The giant clam obtains most of its food from the
single-celled algae that live in the outer tissue of
its mantle. These algae give the mantle of the giant clam its colour.
The algae use energy from the Sun to make food for the clam, and
the clam provides protection and shelter for the algae. Both the
clam and the algae benefit from the relationship. The clam will
die if there are no algae, or if it is kept in the dark. If the algae
have no light they cannot make the food. The 'windows' in the
mantle of the clam are thought to let in more light for the algae.
The giant clam is also a filter feeder, using its ctenidia (see page
22) to sift food
from the water.

▶ The clam uses its
powerful muscles to open
and close the two halves of
the shell. These muscles are
a source of food for people
living on the islands of the
South Pacific.

Reproduction

Reproduction in giant clams occurs when male and female sex cells are released into the sea. **Fertilization** takes place in the open water and the fertilized eggs develop into veliger **larvae** (see page 6). The larvae swim and feed in the open water until they are big enough to settle on sand or part of the reef and begin their adult life fixed in one place.

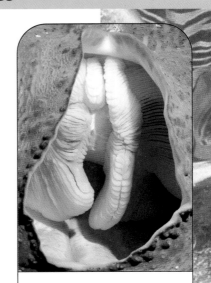

▲ The giant clam is a filter feeder. A current of water is drawn into the clam's body and tiny **organisms** are sifted from the water by its **gills**.

◄ The exposed mantle of the giant clam contains large numbers of tiny algae that make food for the clam.

Amazing facts

- A giant clam found on the Great Barrier Reef off the coast of Australia measured 1 metre across and was estimated to weigh about 250 kilograms.

- Many people believe that a giant clam can snap shut very quickly, trapping divers by their legs and causing them to drown. In fact, clams close their valves quite slowly and there are no real cases of humans being trapped by them.

Cephalopods

Cephalopod means 'head-foot' and describes the position of the head being surrounded by the foot. Cephalopods have **adapted** to become fast-moving **predators**, with highly developed sense organs. Most **species**, with the exception of the nautilus (see pages 34–35), appear very different from **primitive molluscs**. Scientists believe that the **ancestors** of the octopus, squid and cuttlefish **evolved** from nautilus-like forms about 438 million years ago, before there were fish in the sea and trees on land.

Cephalopods are all found in marine habitats, from warm, **tropical** waters to polar regions. Squid live mainly in the open sea, but most cuttlefish and octopuses prefer the seabed close to the shore. There are open-ocean octopuses, though, such as the giant Pacific octopus, found at depths of 750 metres. Nautiluses are mostly found in deep, tropical waters.

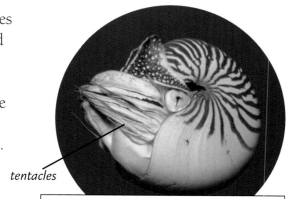

tentacles

▲ The nautilus differs from other cephalopods in having many more tentacles surrounding the mouth. These tentacles do not have suckers.

Classification key

PHYLUM	Mollusca
CLASS	**Cephalopoda**
SUB-CLASS	2 – Coleoidea (octopuses, squid and cuttlefish) and nautiloidea (nautiluses)
ORDERS	5
SPECIES	about 660

▼ The internal shell (cuttlebone) of the cuttlefish is a **buoyancy** organ, which helps the animal to keep its position in the water.

◀ During the day, octopuses hide amongst the rocks. They can use the suckers on their arms to grip the rock and pull themselves along.

Cephalopod features

Cephalopods are **carnivores**, feeding on fish, **crustaceans** and other molluscs that they catch with their **tentacles** (often referred to as arms). The cephalopods range in size from male argonauts with a length of 10 millimetres to the giant squid that can grow to about 20 metres.

The **characteristic** features of the cephalopods include the presence of tentacles (or arms) with suckers, well-developed eyes, a **radula**, and a pair of jaws that form a beak-like mouth. The head is large and surrounded by tentacles, which are used to search for and capture **prey**. The tentacles are formed from the front part of the foot.

Amazing facts

- The cuttlebone from cuttlefish is sold in pet shops as a source of calcium for birds.

- Many cephalopods have special cells called chromatophores in their skin. These cells allow the cephalopod to change its colour and blend into its background to escape from predators.

- Most cephalapods have well-developed eyes with a single lens. Their eyes can form clear, sharp images. The eye of a nautilus does not have a lens. It works like a pinhole camera and can only form a dim image.

Mating follows a complicated courtship. The female lays **fertilized** eggs with large yolks. There are no free-swimming **larval** stages and the young hatch as miniature adults.

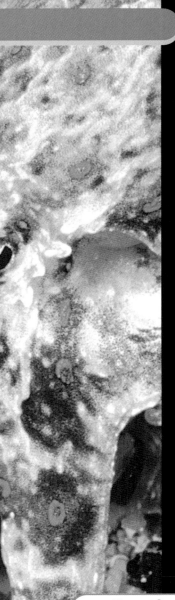

The octopus

Octopuses are found in all the oceans of the world, but they are most common in **tropical** and sub-tropical seas. Most octopuses live on the seabed, where they hunt **crustaceans** and other **molluscs**. The smallest octopus, *Octopus micropyrsus*, has a body length of only 10–25 millimetres, while the body length of some octopuses found in the North Pacific may exceed 1 metre.

Octopus features

Octopuses have eight **tentacles**, or arms, set around a beak-like mouth. They differ from other **cephalopods**, such as squid and cuttlefish, in not having a pair of extra-long arms. Octopuses creep about on the seabed, using the suckers on their arms to grip the rocks. When they need to move quickly, they swim backwards by squirting water out of their funnel.

Octopuses have well-developed brains, excellent eyesight and a great sense of touch, but there is no evidence to suggest that they can react to sound. Their eyes are similar in structure to the eyes of **vertebrates**, with a large lens forming clear images on a part of the eye called the retina. In the vertebrate eye, the image is brought into focus by changing the shape of the lens. In the eye of the octopus, the image is brought into focus by the lens moving backwards and forwards in the eyeball.

Classification key

PHYLUM	Mollusca
CLASS	Cephalopoda
SUB-CLASS	Coleoidea
ORDER	Dibranchiata
SUB-ORDER	Octopoda
FAMILY	Octopodidae
GENUS	*Octopus and others, including Eledone and Cirrothauma*
SPECIES	150

▼ The body of an octopus is short and rounded and there is no internal shell. The arms have two rows of suckers on the under surface.

Masters of disguise

Octopuses can change colour quickly, due to special cells called chromatophores, in their skin. An octopus has two kinds of chromatophore – one kind varies from black to red-brown and the other kind varies from red to orange-yellow. Combinations of these colours mean that an octopus can blend in with its background and escape **predators**. If disturbed, the octopus can also release a dark, inky fluid into the water. This hides it from the predator and gives it time to escape.

Amazing facts

- The largest giant Pacific octopus ever caught weighed 270 kilograms and had an arm span of about 10 metres.

- The female common octopus lays between 200,000 and 400,000 tiny eggs at a time, of which only one or two will survive to become adults.

- When kept in aquariums, octopuses have shown the ability to solve problems by trial and error, such as finding food in a maze. Once a problem has been solved, they can remember it and are able to solve similar problems.

▼ The blue-ringed octopus has a **venomous** bite. This small octopus reaches about 10 centimetres in length and is found off the coast of Australia. It feeds on crabs and prawns.

▲ The paper nautilus is an octopus that looks like a nautilus. Breeding females have thin shells in which the **fertilized** eggs are looked after.

Cuttlefish and squid

Like all **cephalopods**, cuttlefish and squid are **carnivorous**. They all have a beak-like mouth surrounded by eight short **tentacles**, or arms, and two longer ones used for catching **prey**. They have an internal shell, a **radula** and a **streamlined** body with fins along the sides. They use the fins for swimming, but can also move more rapidly by forcing water through the funnel.

Cuttlefish

Cuttlefish live on the seabed fairly close to the shore. They prefer sandy areas, in which they can bury themselves during the day, coming out at night to hunt. The shell of the cuttlefish, called the cuttlebone, is contained within the **mantle**. Extra layers are added to the cuttlebone throughout the life of the cuttlefish. The cuttlebone has hollows in it that are filled with gas and fluids, and it works as a **buoyancy** organ. The proportions of gas and fluid can be controlled by the cuttlefish, allowing it to hover at a certain depth while looking for prey. The cuttlebone also provides a place for muscle attachment and gives support to the body.

Cuttlefish have shorter, broader bodies than squid. The body is slightly flattened from top to bottom. Extending down the side of the body are paired fins, used when swimming slowly. The inner surfaces of the short tentacles and the ends of the elongated ones are covered in short, round suckers.

Classification key	
PHYLUM	Mollusca
CLASS	Cephalopoda
SUB-CLASS	Coleoidea
ORDER	**Sepioida (cuttlefish)**
FAMILIES	5
SPECIES	about 150
ORDER	**Teuthoida (squid)**
FAMILIES	12
SPECIES	about 500

▼ The lateral fins on either side of the body of the cuttlefish are used in swimming.

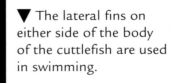

Squid

Squid are more powerful swimmers than cuttlefish and live in the open seas, often at great depths. They have torpedo-shaped, streamlined bodies with diamond-shaped fins at the rear end. The internal shell is a horny structure, called a pen, and is found under the mantle on the upper surface of the animal.

Many **species** of squid have bodies less than 25 centimetres long, but the giant squid, *Architeuthis harveyi*, may reach lengths of 18 metres (including tentacles) and weigh up to 900 kilograms. Giant squid have been seen in the Pacific and North Atlantic Oceans. They are thought to live at the bottom of the ocean, feeding on fish, **crustaceans** and other, smaller squid. Many squid species hunt alone but some, such as the Pacific squid, may hunt in shoals.

Amazing facts

- Like the octopus, squid and cuttlefish can change colour to blend in with their background and will release an inky-black fluid if disturbed.
- Some species of squid living near the surface have been observed to shoot out of the water and glide for distances of up to 45 metres.
- The eyes of the giant squid are the largest in the animal kingdom, measuring up to 25 centimetres in diameter.

▼ Squid have more torpedo-shaped bodies than cuttlefish.

▼ Cuttlefish have eight short tentacles, or arms, and two that are elongated. The elongated tentacles have broader ends and can be moved rapidly. Prey is caught and held by the suckers on the ends of these longer tentacles and then drawn towards the mouth.

The nautilus

The Nautiloidea are an ancient group of **cephalopods** and *Nautilus* is the only surviving genus. It is the only genus of cephalopods with an external shell. At present, there are five **species** found in the warm, **tropical** waters of the Indian and Pacific Oceans. They rest on the ocean bottom during the day and swim around at night catching their **prey**, which consists of small **crustaceans**, such as shrimp, and small fish. Like other cephalopods, they swim by using jet propulsion (see page 13).

▶ The nautilus is found in the Pacific and Indian Oceans.

Classification key

PHYLUM	Mollusca
CLASS	Cephalopoda
SUB-CLASS	Nautiloidea
ORDER	Nautilida
FAMILY	1 – Nautilidae
GENUS	***Nautilus***
SPECIES	5

Many tentacles

The nautilus is similar to other cephalopods in having a head with **tentacles** around the mouth, beak-like jaws and a **radula**. It differs from other cephalopods in having many more tentacles – up to 90 in two rows. These tentacles are small, sticky and able to contract, but they do not have suckers. The eyes of the nautilus are large, but they are simple and do not have a lens. Around the eyes are sensitive tentacles, called ocular tentacles. These are sensitive to touch and protect the eyes.

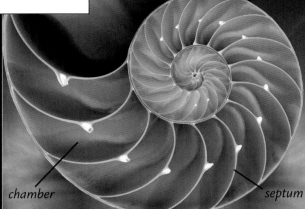

▶ This cutaway view of the shell shows the chambers that have been added as the nautilus has grown.

chamber   *septum*

The nautilus' shell

The shell of the nautilus is smooth and coiled, and can grow to a diameter of 28 centimetres. The shell is lined with mother-of-pearl (nacre), and consists of a number of gas-filled chambers. The animal occupies the outermost, largest chamber of its shell. A speckled, fleshy hood above the head covers part of the shell. When the head is withdrawn into the shell, the hood covers the opening and protects the animal from **predators**.

As the nautilus grows, more chambers are added to the shell, formed by the **mantle**. The previous chamber is sealed off by a wall, called a septum. When a chamber is first sealed off, it is completely filled with fluid. This fluid is gradually replaced by a mixture of gases. The nautilus can vary the amounts of gases and fluids in the chambers of its shell to change its **buoyancy**.

Amazing facts

- The shell of the nautilus is incredibly strong and can withstand pressures of up to 56 kilograms per square centimetre, which is more than five times greater than normal atmospheric pressure.
- About 510 million years ago, the **ancestors** of the nautilus were the largest predators in the seas.

▶ The nautilus feeds on shrimp and fish, which it catches with its tentacles.

Minor classes of molluscs

The most familiar **molluscs**, such as slugs and snails, mussels and octopuses, belong to the three major classes: Gastropoda, Bivalvia and Cephalopoda. In these classes there are many different **species** and some of the species have very large populations. The minor classes have both fewer species and smaller populations. All the species are marine. The Monoplacophora were believed to be **extinct** until the middle of the 20th century and, together with the Aplacophora and Scaphopoda, contain only a few species. The minor classes show us how varied the phylum is and also show how the groups have **evolved** in different ways. This is why it is so difficult to build up a picture of a 'typical' mollusc.

Aplacophorans

These marine molluscs are worm-like, with poorly developed heads, no eyes and no shells. They are covered in a tough sheath, which has tiny, chalky crystals in it. Aplacophorans have no foot or **mantle**, but they do have a **radula**. They live on the seabed or in **coral** reefs. Some species are **predators** and others feed on particles of plants and dead animals. Their size ranges from 1 millimetre to 30 centimetres. Some scientists divide this class into two, the solenogasters and the caudofoveatans. Solenogasters are worm-like molluscs that live in the deep sea and are often found around corals. Caudofoveatans are burrowers that feed on small animals and on decaying plants and animals.

Classification key

PHYLUM	Mollusca
CLASS	**Aplacophora (or Solenogasters and Caudofoveata)**
ORDERS	3
FAMILIES	24
SPECIES	about 250

▼ With their external shell of eight overlapping plates, chitons are thought to resemble **ancestral** molluscs.

Amazing facts

- *Cryptochiton stelleri* is found in the waters from Northern California to Alaska, USA. It is the world's largest species of chiton and can reach a length of about 30 centimetres.
- Tusk shells of the genus *Dentalium* were used as money by the Native Americans of the Pacific coast until the 19th century.

Monoplacophorans

Monoplacophorans were thought to have become extinct more than 300 million years ago. In May 1952 a Danish research ship hauled up a number of living specimens off the coast of Mexico. Since then, a number of different species have been found. Monoplacophorans are small, **primitive** molluscs, ranging in length from 3 to 30 millimetres. They have a cap-like shell and a muscular foot. The shell is very thin, with a mother-of-pearl inner surface and a yellowish-white outer surface. Inside, these molluscs show signs of division into segments, which has led some scientists to believe that molluscs might have evolved from marine annelids (segmented worms).

Classification key

PHYLUM	Mollusca
CLASS	**Monoplacophora**
ORDERS	1
FAMILIES	1
SPECIES	11

Polyplacophorans (chitons)

Chitons are marine molluscs that live in the **intertidal zone** of rocky shores. They feed on algae, which they scrape off the rocks with their radula. They have a flattened, oval shape and a shell made up of eight overlapping plates, or valves, surrounded by a supporting outer ring formed by the mantle.

Classification key

PHYLUM	Mollusca
CLASS	**Polyplacophora (chitons)**
ORDERS	3
FAMILIES	13
SPECIES	about 600

Scaphopods (tusk shells)

This class of marine molluscs lives on the seabed in sand or mud. They have elongated, tubular shells that are open at both ends. The head is not well developed and they have no eyes or **tentacles**. The adults move about searching for food with their heads buried in the sand or mud. Food is caught using fine, needle-like filaments covered in **cilia**. These filaments can tighten in order to move food into the mouth, where there is a large radula.

Classification key

PHYLUM	Mollusca
CLASS	**Scaphopoda (tusk shells)**
ORDERS	2
FAMILIES	8
SPECIES	550

► Tusk shells have elongated bodies with reduced heads and spend their lives feeding on plant and animal remains on the seabed.

Molluscs under threat

Many **molluscs** are under threat of becoming **extinct**. It is thought that 34 **species** of **bivalve** and 264 species of **gastropod** have become extinct since the mid-20th century. More than 50 species of bivalve and 170 species of gastropod have been listed as 'critically endangered' by the World Conservation Union (IUCN).

Coral reefs are home to many marine molluscs. In places where supplies of wood or stone for building are limited, coral reefs are sometimes broken up to provide building materials. Reefs are also damaged by snorkellers and divers, and polluted by sewage and oil spills.

Pollution of the oceans by sewage and industrial wastes is a serious problem. In many parts of the world, waste is dumped into the sea and leakages occur from underwater pipelines. Oil spills from tankers and underwater pipelines destroy **organisms**, and poisonous chemicals getting into the water can build up in **food chains**.

Similar problems affect molluscs in freshwater habitats. Pesticides, herbicides and fertilizers – chemicals used in farming to kill insect pests and weeds, and to produce more crops – can run off fields into streams and ponds. Molluscs can be killed directly by chemical pollution, or be affected by changes in the food chain. Changes such as the draining of marshes to provide more farmland can mean that important habitats for molluscs are destroyed.

▼ Large shells are removed from coral reefs to satisfy the demand from collectors.

Hunting and collecting

Sea shells are collected by many people to be made into ornaments and jewellery. They have even been used instead of money. Most shells sold in shops to collectors have been taken from living animals. If too many molluscs are removed from one place, such as a coral reef, there is a danger of species becoming extinct. This is a particular threat to molluscs such as nautiluses, helmet shells and murexes because people are especially keen to collect the bigger, more unusual shells.

Over-harvesting of molluscs for food is a threat to certain species. Mussels, clams, scallops and oysters are amongst the most popular bivalves eaten by humans.

▶ The shells for sale here were probably taken illegally from living animals.

Introduced species

The introduction, by humans, of one species to control the numbers of another species in an area can disrupt populations within **ecosystems**. For example, zebra mussels, which were introduced into North America from Eastern Europe, reproduce much faster than native mussels and compete for food and living space. They can kill the native mussels by holding their shells closed to stop them taking in oxygen and food.

Amazing facts

- Oysters and other bivalves formed part of the diet of prehistoric man. Large mounds of shells have been found in many coastal areas near prehistoric settlements around the world.
- Cone shells are prized for their beautiful patterns, but collectors are in danger from the poisonous teeth if they attempt to collect live specimens.

◀ Zebra mussels do not appear to have any natural enemies, or to be sensitive to poor water conditions. Therefore, they can thrive in areas where other mussel species may die out.

Protecting molluscs

There are many ways in which it is possible to prevent **molluscs** from becoming **extinct**. In order to protect them, it is important to protect their natural habitats, and study the stages of their life cycles and the foods they eat. Some molluscs are considered pests and it is important to make sure that the steps taken to control them do not disrupt **food chains** or interfere with habitats.

Marine sanctuaries and guided trips to coastal areas, such as **coral** reefs, all help to inform people of the importance of preserving **aquatic** habitats. The conservation of coral reefs, limiting the collection of molluscs for their shells, and controlling the activities of divers can reduce the threat to endangered **species**.

◀ Guided trips to coral reefs help to protect the environment of endangered species.

Breeding programmes

One way of conserving endangered species is to breed them in captivity and then release them back into their natural habitat. Many species of *Partula* snails, native snails of the South Pacific islands, are listed as endangered. There have been a number of attempts to breed these snails in captivity. In 1994, the London Zoological Society released the first *Partula* snails bred in captivity into a protected area on one of the South Pacific islands. These snails had to be protected from the **carnivorous** snails living there, so that they stood a chance of reproducing in the wild and building up the population. The numbers of the *Partula* snails are counted regularly in order to monitor the long-term success of the project.

◀ Abalones are easy to collect but over-harvesting has led to their being threatened with extinction.

Laws

Laws and agreements can ban the killing of certain species or limit the number that can be caught. This type of conservation can be useful in keeping up the numbers of certain species of molluscs. In California, USA, strict laws control the abalone industry in order to prevent the extinction of this mollusc. It is illegal to remove abalones under a minimum length. This gives the abalones time to reach maturity and reproduce before they are collected. A ban on the export of abalone meat from the state of California means that the number of people who can buy it is limited, and this discourages people from collecting abalones to sell.

Amazing facts

- Abalones take a long time to reach maturity. They are not able to reproduce until they are six years old. Many are collected before they reach this age, which has contributed to the decline in their numbers.

- Soft-shelled clams are caught for food. In the USA, the legal harvest size is about 5 centimetres in diameter. Any smaller clams that are caught must be replaced.

◀ Amber snails in some parts of the world are under threat from introduced species of snail that compete for food and space.

Classification

Scientists have found and classified about 2 million different types of animals. With so many **species** it is important that they are classified into groups. The groups show how living **organisms** are related by **evolution** and where they belong in the natural world. A scientist identifies an animal by looking at its features, for example, by counting the number of legs or what teeth it has. Animals that share the same features belong to the same species. Species with similar **characteristics** are placed in the same genus. The genera are grouped together in families, families are grouped into orders and orders are grouped into classes. Classes are grouped together in phyla (singular: phylum) and finally, phyla are grouped into kingdoms. Kingdoms are the largest groups and are at the highest level. There are five kingdoms: monerans (bacteria), protists (single-celled organisms), fungi, plants and animals.

Naming an animal

Each species has a unique scientific name, usually called its Latin name, consisting of two words. The first word is the name of the genus to which the organism belongs and the second is the name of its species. For example, the Latin name of the marble cone shell is *Conus marmoreus* and that of the striated cone shell is *Conus striatus*. This tells us that these animals are grouped in the same genus but are different species. Latin names are used to avoid confusion. Abalones, **gastropods** found off the west coast of North America, are called ormers, awabis or ear-shells depending on where you happen to be. Sometimes there are very small differences between individuals that belong to the same species, so there is an extra division called a sub-species. To show that an animal belongs to a sub-species, another name is added to the end of the Latin name. For example, there are two sub-species of the snail *Partula suturalis* – *Partula suturalis strigosa* and *Partula suturalis vexillum*.

▼ There are many species of snail but they share common features of a spiral shell and muscular foot.

This table shows how a common limpet is classified.

Classification	Example: common limpet	Features
Kingdom	Animalia	Common limpets belong to the animal kingdom because they have many cells, need to eat food and are formed from a **fertilized** egg.
Phylum	Mollusca	A common limpet is a **mollusc** because it has a shell, a muscular foot and a **radula**.
Class	Gastropoda	A common limpet is a gastropod because it has a single-valved shell, a head with **tentacles** and a well-developed foot used in crawling.
Sub-class	Prosobranchia	Common limpets are prosobranchs because they are marine snails with a shell, a **mantle cavity**, **gills** and one pair of tentacles on the head.
Order	Archaeogastropoda	Common limpets belong to this order because they **browse** on algae and have very strong shells, which can be clamped down on to the rocks. They have numerous rows of teeth on the radula and a shiny lining to the shell.
Family	Patellidae	Members of this family have conical, ribbed shells and are found on rocky shores.
Genus	*Patella*	A genus is a group of species that are more closely related to one another than to any other members of a family. *Patella* is the genus for the common limpet.
Species	*vulgata*	A species is a group of individuals that can **interbreed** successfully. *Patella vulgata* is the complete name for the common limpet.

Mollusc evolution

About 35,000 **fossil species** of **molluscs** have been identified and described. Mollusc fossils are found in sedimentary, or layered, rocks, such as limestone, chalk and clay. Fossilized shells are common in the limestone used for buildings and it is also possible to find shells and impressions of shells in exposed rocks on mountains and cliffs.

Molluscs first appeared about 580 million years ago, and by 500 million years ago, **gastropods**, **bivalves** and **cephalopods** had **evolved** and were around in great numbers. Molluscs were common in most marine **ecosystems**. The next major event in the history of mollusc **evolution** occurred about 400 million years ago, when some of the bivalves became **adapted** to life in fresh water. The first land snails appeared 350 million years ago, when green plants began to grow across large areas of the Earth's surface.

The fossil record shows that a great number of different mollusc types evolved but many became **extinct** millions of years ago. It is not possible to trace direct relationships between the living groups of molluscs or to determine a common **ancestor** with any certainty.

▲ For 125 million years ammonites were the dominant marine animals. They became extinct 100 million years ago. With their flat spiral shells, there is a resemblance to some present-day molluscs.

▼ The coiled shell of the snail evolved in response to the increase in the size of the body.

present-day molluscs

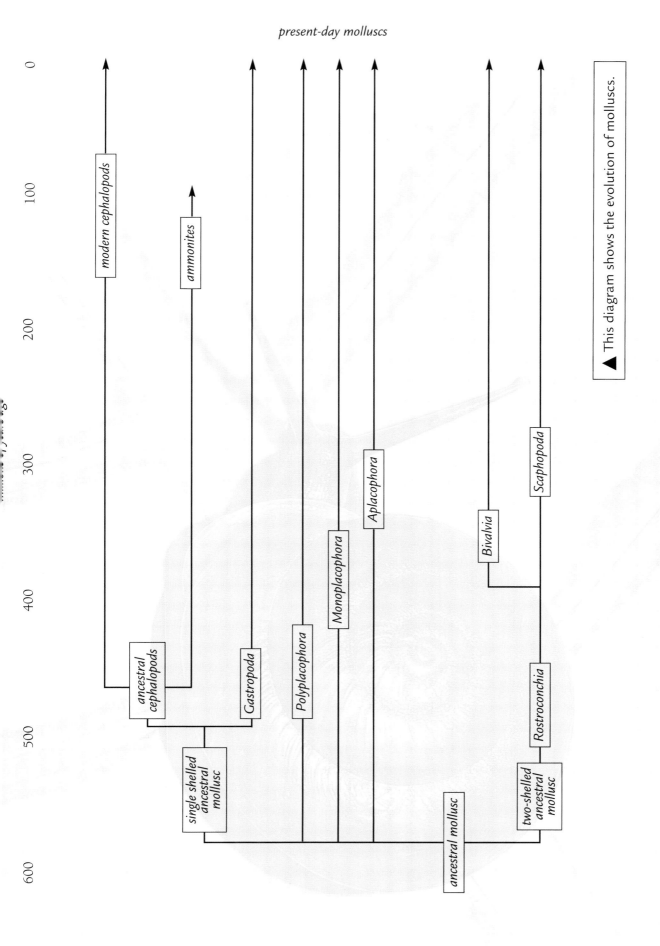

▲ This diagram shows the evolution of molluscs.

Glossary

adapt change in order to cope with the environment

aestivation period of inactivity in hot or dry weather

ancestor individual from which an animal is descended

appendage outgrowth of the body used for feeding or movement

aquatic living in water

arthropod member of the phylum Arthropoda, with jointed appendages and a segmented body, such as an insect or spider

bivalve mollusc with a shell in two parts

browser mollusc that feeds on plant material

buoyancy ability to float

camouflage colours and patterns that let an animal blend with its surroundings

carnivore animal that eats other animals

cephalopod mollusc with sucker-bearing tentacles or arms

characteristic feature or quality of an animal, for example having a shell or radula

cilia tiny, hair-like structures found on the gills of molluscs; they beat rhythmically, setting up currents and moving mucus

coral small sea animal that catches food by using its stinging tentacles. Coral live in large colonies called coral reefs.

crustacean arthropod that has antennae, eyes on stalks and a shield-like covering over the head and thorax

ecosystem community of organisms and their interaction with the environment

evolution slow process of change in living organisms so that they can adapt to their environment

evolve change very slowly over a long period of time

extinct no longer in existence; to have permanently disappeared or died out

fertilize coming together of an egg (from a female) and sperm (from a male) to form a new individual

food chain organisms that are linked because they depend on each other for food. For example, a plant may be eaten by a slug, which in turn is eaten by a bird.

fossil preserved remains of an organism that lived millions of years ago

gastropod class of molluscs with a broad foot and a single shell, such as a snail

gill organ used to obtain oxygen from water for use in vital body processes

grazer mollusc that feeds on plant material

herbivore animal that eats plants

hermaphrodite animal that has both male and female sex organs

host living organism whose body provides food for a parasite

interbreed mate with another animal of the same species

intertidal zone area on a shore that lies between the highest and lowest points reached by the tides

invertebrate animal that does not have a backbone

larva (plural: **larvae**) young animal that looks different from the adult and changes shape as it develops

ligament tough band of tissue that connects bones or supports muscles

lung body organ through which oxygen is absorbed from the air

mantle outer fold of skin lining the mantle cavity, covering the hump containing the body organs and producing the shell if there is one

mantle cavity in molluscs, a cavity, or space, between the mantle and the rest of the body; in aquatic molluscs, this cavity is filled with water and contains the gills

mate (verb) join with a member of the opposite sex so that male sex cells (sperm) can fertilize female sex cells (eggs) in order to produce new individuals

membrane thin sheet of body tissue

mollusc invertebrate with, most typically, a head, a muscular foot and an external shell

mucus sticky fluid produced by animals; it moistens and protects body organs

omnivore animal that eats both plants and animals

operculum cover used to seal a gastropod's shell when the animal has withdrawn inside

organism individual plant or animal

parasite organism that spends part or all of its life obtaining food and shelter from another organism's body

predator animal that catches and kills other animals for food

prey animal that is caught and killed by other animals for food

primitive at an early stage of development or evolution. For example, chitons are more primitive than gastropods.

radula (plural: **radulae**) thin sheet of body tissue covered with rows of teeth

sea anemone animal with a cup-shaped body and a ring of tentacles around the mouth. It attaches itself to rocks.

siphon tube used for drawing in or emptying out liquid

species group of individuals that share many characteristics and can interbreed to produce offspring

streamlined shaped to allow smooth movement through water or air

tentacles in gastropods, small sense organs that are attached to the head; in cephalopods, the front part of the foot, which has suckers and is used for catching prey

tropical relating to the tropics – hot regions of the world between the tropic of Cancer and the tropic of Capricorn

venom poison

vertebrate animal with a backbone

Further information

BOOKS TO READ

Burnie, David (ed.), *Animal: the Definitive Guide to the World's Wildlife* (Dorling Kindersley Ltd, 2001)

Burton, Maurice and Robert, *The Encyclopedia of Insects and Invertebrates* (Silverdale Books, 2002) (Adapted from *The Little Brown Encyclopedia of Animals*)

Macquitty, Dr Miranda, *Eyewitness Ocean* (Dorling Kindersley Ltd, 2003)

Parker, Steve, *Eyewitness Seashore* (Dorling Kindersley Ltd, 2003)

WEBSITES

http://animaldiversity.ummz.umich.edu
Website of the Museum of Zoology, University of Michigan, with detailed information on all animal groups, including molluscs.

http://coa.acnatsci.org/conchnet/edushell.html
Conchologists of America. A website specially designed for people interested in molluscs and collecting shells.

http://www.bbc.co.uk/nature
Find information on all kinds of animals from invertebrates to mammals.

http://www.ucmp.berkeley.edu/mollusca
The University of California, Berkeley. This website has detailed information on mollusc groups and specific examples.

Index